ANDREW'S AWESOME ADVENTURES WITH HIS ADHD BRAIN

Helping Children and Parents to Understand Inattentive-type ADHD

Kristin M. Wilcox, Ph.D.

With Andrew S. Wilcox

Illustrated by Sean Maykrantz

For information, contact
MSI Press LLC
1760-F Airline Hwy, #203
Hollister, CA 95023

Illustrations: Sean Maykrantz and Andrew S. Wilcox
Copyeditor: Betty Lou Leaver
Cover Design: Sean Maykrantz and Opeyemi Ikuborije
Layout: Opeyemi Ikuborije

ISBN: 978-1-957354-02-6
LCCN: 2022900986

For all the creative, risk-taking, whirlwinds of disorganization and emotional outbursts. Without you, the world would be less interesting. For all the family, educators, and professionals who helped Andrew with his ADHD.

CONTENTS

PART II - KRISTIN'S STORY

Acknowledgements

First and foremost, I want to thank Andrew, my inspiration for writing this book. I could not have pursued writing the book without the encouragement and support of my husband, Scott, my son, Matthew, and my mom and dad who all participated in countless discussions about the book and inattentive-type ADHD. A special thank you to my brother, Rick Sonntag, who helped this scientific writer hone her creative writing skills to be able to tell Andrew's story.

Thanks to Dr. Mark Riddle at Johns Hopkins University School of Medicine who alerted me to the lack of information on the inattentive subtype of ADHD in boys, and to all the ADHD researchers who graciously sent me copies of their research articles when I requested them. Early discussions with Stephanie Sobchak helped to spark the idea for the book. She also recommended my fantastic illustrator, Sean Maykrantz and connected me with author Mia Crews who advised me as a first-time book author. Rick, Mia, and Amy Navarre all read and provided valuable comments on the manuscript proposal.

Thanks to executive editor Betty Lou Leaver at San Juan Books, and to her amazing team who helped to turn my idea into a reality.

Finally, I want to thank all the kids, parents and caregivers who picked up this book and read it. Hopefully we can all continue to learn about and understand the inattentive subtype of ADHD.

PART I
Andrew's Story

This is a brain.

This is my brain.

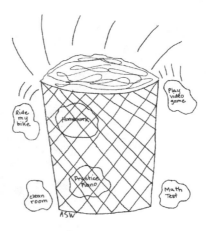

A Disorganized Heaping Disaster (ADHD)

1

"Do what you can, with what you have, where you are."

President Theodore Roosevelt

<u>A</u>lways <u>D</u>isorganized and <u>H</u>opelessly <u>D</u>istracted (ADHD)

Blink, blink, blink, the cursor keeps time on the blank screen as thoughts rush through my brain like a runaway freight train.

"What was that book about? Who were the characters?"

Oh, where to begin? There are just too many details to think about. My thoughts drift aimlessly as I stare out of my bedroom window. It's a sunny day, and there is the smell of freshly cut grass pulling my attention to what I could be doing. I wish I were riding my bike or fishing down at the stream. Instead, here I am stuck at my desk, writing a dreaded book report for English class.

Correction, I am *not* writing it. I wish I could *make* myself write it. If I were writing it, then I could be done with it. All I want is to be done with it. Why didn't I start working on it when it was assigned to us weeks ago? "Ugh!"

Now, it's the night before the report is due. Why do I always wait until the last minute? Characters, setting, and theme. Chug-a-lug like that freight train going through my head, keeping time with the blinking cursor on the still blank screen. My brain hurts. How do I get it all organized? Where's the book? "Ouch!" Stupid Legos scattered all over my bedroom floor. Mom told me to clean those up yesterday. Under my bed, I find some dirty socks, random puzzle pieces, and a wrapper from a granola bar. "Oh, I got it; I found the book!" Never mind, it's not the one for my book report; it's the paper airplane book I have been missing.

"What page was that airplane on I wanted to make?" flipping through the paper airplane book, I hear someone talking off in the distance.

"Andrew, are you working on your book report? You know it's due tomorrow." Mom's talking to me.

I sit back down at my desk. Maybe if I sit here and think about it, I can remember where that book is. I keep eyeing the paper airplane book on the floor and ask why do we need to write about books in 7th grade anyway? I hear Mom's voice in my head, "Andrew, learning to write is an important skill that you will need in high school and even college." Blah, blah, blah. I struggle with writing; it has been like that for as long as I can remember. In elementary school, countless half-finished worksheets got shoved into my desk. Now, in middle school one-page essays on random, boring topics turned into full-blown book reports. We don't even get to write about something cool, like traveling in outer space or building a habitat on Mars.

"Writing is agony, plain and simple."

When I was eight and in third grade, I was diagnosed with Attention Deficit Hyperactivity Disorder, or ADHD. I finally had an explanation why I struggled with writing and had difficulty paying attention sometimes. I like to think of my ADHD as an elephant living in my brain. It is big and imposing, and it gets in the way.

When the English teacher hands back our graded book reports, I just stare at the paper I have left face down on the desk, not wanting to turn it over to see the grade. Finally, I make myself flip the paper over. There it is, the letter "D" written across the top in red marker, with a note from the teacher, "Andrew, I know you can do better." If only that paper airplane book weren't in my room.

* * *

Did you know?

ADHD has been diagnosed in kids since the 1770s, around the time that the Declaration of Independence was signed. There are three types of ADHD:

1. Inattentive Subtype: Some kids with ADHD have trouble paying attention, like me. We also have trouble listening to others, following instructions, staying organized, keeping track of our stuff, doing something we have to pay attention to for a long period of time (homework, cleaning our bedrooms), and remembering things we are supposed to do every day (brushing teeth, turning in homework). Sometimes, when my brain doesn't want to pay attention, I end up folding paper airplanes instead of writing my book report.

2. Hyperactive Subtype: Some kids with ADHD have trouble sitting still, playing quietly, and waiting their turn; they are always on the go, talk a lot, and interrupt others. Even though I sometimes butt into conversations, I am not considered hyperactive.

3. Combined Subtype: Some kids with ADHD have several behaviors associated with inattention and hyperactivity. This subtype is the one most diagnosed in children.

Kristin M. Wilcox, Ph.D. with Andrew S. Wilcox

2

"ADHD: Have more thoughts before breakfast than most people have all day."

Author Unknown

My ADHD Brain Made Me Do It

I like science. There are no writing essays, and we get to do cool lab experiments. I get good grades in science and can pay attention in class—most of the time, anyway. Today we are learning about the brain. I stare at a diagram of the brain up on the board and listen while my teacher explains what the different parts of the brain do.

"Every day our brains are bombarded with thousands of pieces of information from the world around us," she says. "The *frontal cortex* is like a military force keeping out the enemy, only letting in the information you need to pay attention to at the time. The frontal cortex is responsible for you being able to learn, remember, plan, organize, pay attention, and control your emotions." Apparently, my ADHD frontal cortex is less military-like and more laid-back-on-vacation-like, making my brain feel like an overstuffed garbage can with a lid that doesn't stay on and garbage falling all over the floor.

The teacher drones on endlessly with the lesson. Glancing out the window, I see the eighth graders on the playground, playing basketball during recess. I wish I was out at recess instead of being stuck in class.

"Andrew, are you paying attention?" The teacher is asking me a question. I am snapped back into science class with a sudden feeling of dread in the pit of my stomach. What did she ask me? I was thinking about basketball! I stare at her with a blank look on my face. I slump in my chair as she selects another victim to answer the question. I wish paying attention in class weren't such a struggle.

The teacher hands out an assignment with questions about our lesson on the brain. Tap, tap, tap. The kid next to me tapping his pencil on the desk is so annoying. What is the teacher saying? I try to ignore the drumming in my brain.

"Okay, class, it's time to start your assignment."

Sigh! Once again, I miss the instructions for the assignment. Reluctantly, I push my chair back and shuffle over to the teacher's desk. I know exactly what she is going to say to me: "Oh, Andrew, you need to listen and pay attention." But the infuriating drumming ADHD elephant in my brain made it impossible for me to concentrate. Her non-ADHD brain doesn't understand.

I walk back to my desk, flop down in the seat, and flip through page after page of the assignment I am supposed to complete. There are too many pages. Oh, where to begin? I don't want to think about the assignment right now. I wonder if the eighth graders are still playing basketball. Once again, I am staring out the window, only to be pulled back into class by the bell ringing, signaling class is *finally* over. Then *panic*! I look down at the pages on my desk to see they are all still blank. The teacher is walking up and down the aisles, collecting our assignment. Why is she walking so fast? I scramble to write something, anything.

The teacher stops at my desk and asks, "Andrew, what have you been doing for the past 20 minutes?"

I almost blurt out, "Twenty minutes? It was more like five minutes!" Then, I look at the clock on the wall and see she is correct. Did I mention my laid-back-on-vacation ADHD brain isn't very good at keeping track of time? I just look at the teacher and shrug my shoulders while thinking my brain made me do it.

* * *

Did you know?

ADHD runs in families. Chances are if you have ADHD, then someone in your family has it, too.

3

"ADHD is not a disability but a different ability."
Author Unknown

Sometimes My ADHD Brain Needs a Reminder on a Neon-Colored Sticky Note.

Dismissal time! My ADHD brain doesn't have to pay attention in school anymore today. Now, if I could only remember what I have for homework. I rummage through the miscellaneous papers shoved into my backpack, looking for my planner. "Found it!" It's blank because I forgot to write down my homework assignments. Again. I stare at the books in my locker hoping to remember. Nope. "Darn!" I hear my bus number being called. Slamming the locker shut, I run down the hall with the nagging feeling I am forgetting something.

I weave in and out of the sea of kids making their way to the front door of the school. My feet are moving faster now as I make the final sprint to the bus. Made it with only a minute to spare!

I flop down onto the seat. "My trumpet! That's what I forgot!" Mom reminded me before I left for school this morning to bring my trumpet home. Oh well, it's not the first time the ADHD elephant has forgotten to bring something home from school. The bus is moving at a snail's pace.

Finally, my stop. Running into the house, I toss my backpack on the kitchen floor and race up the stairs to my room. I head straight for my computer and begin working on the awesome Mars habitat I am building in a game.

The world around me fades away, and I am lost in the game, thinking about being an astronaut and going to Mars.

"Andrew."

"Andrew!"

Mom, standing in the doorway of the bedroom, is calling my name, but I am so engrossed in my game I don't hear her. "It's time to start your homework. Did you write down your assignments in your planner?" she asks.

Mom hands me the planner from my backpack. I sense she already knows I didn't write down my assignments. My planner is filled with a lot of awesome doodles but no homework assignments.

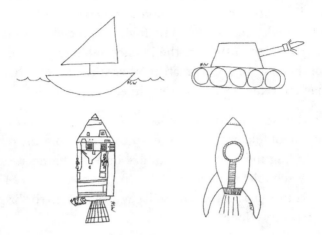

How is my overstuffed garbage-can brain supposed to remember to write down my homework every day? I look from Mom to the blank page of the open planner I am holding and, remembering what my science teacher said about the frontal cortex, tell her, "My brain made me do it." Mom just shakes her head and hands me my backpack.

I know I have a math quiz tomorrow, so I grab my math folder out of the backpack. While continuing to work on the Mars habitat, I aimlessly flip through math worksheets, not really paying attention. They are just a jumble of numbers and words.

I decide to head downstairs to the kitchen for a snack. I'm not particularly hungry. The ADHD elephant just never wants to do boring stuff, like studying.

In the kitchen, I glance out from the pantry and see the blinding color of one of Mom's neon sticky notes, stuck to my folder for school. The folder I needed for school today but left sitting on the kitchen table this morning. Not the first time. Oh great, another sticky note! What do I need to remember to do this time?

Those colorful reminders pop up everywhere—on my school folders, my desk, even the bathroom mirror—reminding me to put my laundry into the hamper, turn in my schoolwork, and practice the piano. I guess Mom thinks the ADHD elephant will pay attention to the bright neon colors. Nope.

"How is your studying going for the math quiz?" Mom asks me as she walks into the kitchen.

"Ugh."

"You should get back to studying since you have an appointment with your counselor this afternoon."

My counselor specializes in helping kids with ADHD. I meet with her once a week, and today we are going to continue working on my ADHD Brain-Busting Strategies, or ABBS, to help me stay focused when my ADHD brain is bored, like when I am studying for a math quiz.

Here I have written down the ABBS I use to help me with my schoolwork.

1. I squeeze a ball in my hand when I need to focus for a long time, like when I take a test in school or have a long homework assignment. My ADHD counselor told me the act of moving my hand to squeeze the ball can increase chemicals in my brain that help me to focus and pay attention. Linking paper clips together, folding paper, or doodling also work. Maybe all the doodles in my planner aren't such a bad thing after all.

2. I have a special folder for homework assignments that need to be turned in to the teacher the following day. Most of the time I can remember to check the folder at the end of the school day to make sure its empty. If it's not, I am sure to find

a neon-colored sticky note on the folder with a reminder to turn in my homework.

3. When I am doing homework, I set a timer for 20 minutes—any longer and my ADHD brain will be going to the kitchen to rummage aimlessly through the pantry for a snack. I try to put all my effort into getting as much work done as I can in 20 minutes. When the timer goes off, I take a short break, around 10-15 minutes, and do something fun, like work on the Mars habitat. Then I set the timer for another round.

After mindlessly staring into the kitchen pantry for who knows how long, I decide to go back to my room, and using my ABBS, I set my timer and start really studying for the math quiz this time.

The next morning I roll over and turn off the obnoxious ringing of my alarm clock; I am not a morning person. Then I count down the days until the weekend. Fumbling around in the dark, I manage to find a t-shirt and pants in the pile of clothes on the floor and get dressed. Ouch! Stupid Legos are still scattered on the floor. I switch on the computer monitor and just as I start to sit down to work on the Mars habitat, I hear my mom, "Andrew come down for breakfast."

Sigh! I never have time to do what I want to do.

"Are you ready for your math quiz?" Mom asks as I flop down in the chair at the kitchen table.

"Ugh." I forgot about the math quiz today.

"Don't forget to take your medicine."

Every morning at breakfast I take medicine for my ADHD to help me focus better in school. My doctor said the medicine keeps the focus chemicals in my brain at the right level so my relaxing-on-vacation frontal cortex operates more like the streamlined military force.

After I am done eating breakfast, I rummage through the mound of crumpled papers in my backpack looking for the squeeze ball I use when I take tests at school. I hear the bus rumbling down our street. Oh, I am sure it's in here somewhere. Time to go!

"Remember to bring your trumpet home today." Mom calls after me as I race out the door to catch the bus. Maybe I will find a neon-colored sticky note on my school folder with a reminder for that.

* * *

Did you know?

ADHD has nothing to do with how smart you are. ADHD brains struggle with something called *working memory*. Working memory helps me keep information in my brain until I need to use it, like when I am solving a math problem. For example, for the math problem 4+5+10, I calculate 4+5=9, then, using working memory to keep the number 9 in my brain, add 10 to get 9 + 10 = 19. Working memory is also important for helping me to pay attention and follow instructions, all those things teachers like me to do.

4

"They say a cluttered desk is a sign of a cluttered mind. What, then, is an empty desk a sign of?"

Albert Einstein

My ADHD Brain Is a Master of Disaster.

My mom is on a constant mission to tame my tornadic ADHD brain.

"Andrew, how can you possibly work at your desk with papers piled everywhere, Legos strewn about, and a stack of empty plates and cups?"

I look up from the computer, survey the desk, and shrug my shoulders. "It's not so bad."

I shove a pile of papers to the side. They teeter on the edge of the desk, fall to the floor, and scatter in every direction covering my carpet in a snow-white blanket.

Oh, there's the instructions for my science project! I haven't started it yet, and it's due the day after tomorrow. I pick the page of instructions up off the floor and put it on top of another pile of papers on my desk. I misplace important papers for school all the time. I turn back to the computer and start playing my game again.

"Mom, why do I have to bother with cleaning off my desk? It's going to stay organized for all of ten minutes. You know me; I'm not organized."

Mom eyes the mess on the floor, then looks up at me. Reluctantly, I get up from my desk and look from the pile of papers on the floor to the pile of papers on my desk. The thought of cleaning up makes my brain ache.

I poke and prod at the things on my desk, pushing stuff around from one place to another. There's the Lego car I built last month! I wondered where I'd left it. I start to wonder if I should I add on some bigger tires? Maybe a new design altogether? I place the car next to the Lego bin on the floor so I can finish it later. I'll finish this later; I'll finish that later. Everything always gets put off until later. I hear Mom walking up the stairs. She is coming to check on my progress. I scramble to clean up the papers scattered on my floor.

"Andrew, you have been up here for an hour. Your desk still has a pile of papers on it the size of Mount Everest, and papers are still all over your floor."

I wish the ADHD elephant was better at keeping track of time. I spot my folder for school on the floor, All of the papers stuffed inside have caused it to rip apart, and now it's covered in random strips of duct tape. I wish duct tape could hold together the mess on my desk.

ABBS

1. BREAKDOWN BIG TASKS INTO SMALLER TASKS

2. MAKE IT EASY TO STORE YOUR STUFF

3. CLEAN UP OR CLEAN OUT ONCE A WEEK

4. LISTEN TO MUSIC WHILE COMPLETING A TASK

are the ABBS I use to help organize my disorganized ADHD brain:

1. I try to break down a big task into very specific parts so my ADHD brain doesn't get overwhelmed. When I clean my room, Mom helps me to make a list of specific tasks:

   - Put all laundry in the hamper.
   - Clean up the Legos off the floor.
   - Make the bed.

2. I use clear bins and open shelves for storage. If my ADHD brain can't easily see where something goes, then it's going on some pile to be found again in a month or two.

3. I try to clean up or, clean out, once a week. Then I don't have to use all of Dad's duct tape to keep my exploding folder for school together.

4. Sometimes, I listen to music. The rhythm of the music helps my ADHD brain by increasing the focus chemicals.

5. If all else fails, Mom keeps her stash of neon-colored sticky notes at hand.

* * *

Did you know?

Inattentive ADHD brains can focus intently on something they like to do. It's called *hyperfocus*. Hyperfocus is something that is good about my ADHD brain. Keep reading, and I will tell you more about it.

Kristin M. Wilcox, Ph.D. with Andrew S. Wilcox

"While we may not be able to control all that happens to us, we can control what happens inside us."

Benjamin Franklin

Monumental Meltdowns and My ADHD Brain

The kid sitting across from me on the bus is picking his nose. I turn away and look out the window, watching the endless line of kids sprint by, trying to make it to their bus on time. Music is blaring from the back of the bus, and kids are talking loudly over the music. A group of eighth grade girls is getting on the bus now and talking nonstop about some cute boy in their science class.

"Hello," I say as they pass by. The lead girl stops dead in her tracks and glares at me. I immediately regret my decision.

"Oh, look at that, the little seventh grader thinks he can talk to us."

All at once, the group of girls begins to laugh and make fun of me. Clenched fists, muscles tensing, heart pounding, and teeth grinding, I feel the anger rising from my toes to the top of my head. I am helpless to stop it.

In a flash, I am yelling as loud as I can, "Stop laughing at me!" The more I yell, the more the girls laugh.

I notice one of the girls is holding a book in her hands. Whap! I knock the book out of the girl's hand and onto the floor of the bus. Now, the girls aren't laughing. I raise my eyes from focusing on the book lying on the floor of the bus to find all the kids staring at me. Embarrassed, I flop back down onto my seat, wishing the bus would get moving already—not the finest moment for me and my lose-control ADHD brain.

That afternoon I tell my ADHD counselor about the incident with the girls on the bus. I feel a little better after she tells me my ADHD can make it difficult for me to control my reaction, temper, and behavior when something makes me angry.

"It's okay to get angry. Even non-ADHD brains get mad, but you have to learn to control your behavior when you get frustrated."

These ABBS help me control my response to frustrating situations:

1. I try to pay attention to how I feel and recognize when I am getting angry and frustrated. My ADHD brain doesn't always think about the consequences of my actions, and sometimes my behavior can be impulsive, like when I slapped

the book out of the eighth-grade girl's hand in front of everyone on the bus.

2. If I feel myself getting angry or frustrated, I try to walk away from the situation. I often use this strategy when I am working on one of my model kits with the tiny pieces that just don't seem to fit right or building with Legos when I can't seem to find a specific piece. This strategy even works for difficult homework assignments.

3. Sometimes, if I can't walk away, I think of someplace I would rather be. The place I like to think about is the Kennedy Space Center in Florida. They have an outdoor area with several rockets towering above you. I like to imagine myself there walking under the giant rockets, looking up trying to see the top.

* * *

Did you know?

Laughing can help when you are angry. The positive effect laughing has on your brain is greater than the negative effect anger has on your brain. Think of how funny your face looks when you are mad, maybe all squished together like a troll, and use that image to help change your anger into laughter. Because what's funnier than a troll face?

6

"Quiet people have the loudest minds."

Stephen Hawking

(Easier said than done with an ADHD elephant
living in your brain.)

My ADHD Brain Doesn't Like
All the Hoopla

My stomach is grumbling. It's been hours since I ate
breakfast. The grumbling seems to be getting louder
and louder, and I can barely pay attention to the English
teacher as she goes on and on about a boring book we are
reading for class. Will the bell for lunch just ring already!
Finally, the bell is shouting out obnoxiously, and kids rush
toward the classroom door, making the mad dash down
to the cafeteria.

Getting to the cafeteria with enough time left to eat
is like running a race. If I get stuck behind the kids in the

math class that always gets out late for lunch, I'll never make it in time. Phew! I just barely made it past their classroom, only to be slowed down by a line of girls who are more concerned with gossiping then making it to the cafeteria. Finally, I squeeze past by them, flying into the cafeteria. I spot my buddies sitting at our regular table, rush over, and sit down.

The noise level in the cafeteria is deafening with kids trying to shout over one another. The ADHD elephant doesn't like all the noise, and it makes my brain hurt. More lunchtime commotion as kids make a mad dash out to the playground. It's quiet now. No more trays banging, no more utensils clanging, no more kids shouting. My friends and I like to stay inside for recess. Excitedly, I ask my friends if they want to hear about the new addition to the Mars habitat in my game. We end up talking about our different computer games for another few minutes until the bell starts its obnoxious ringing again, signaling the end of lunch.

After lunch, the stampede moves much more slowly, crawling like a traffic jam on the highway. My brain is in its post-lunch slump as I walk into social studies and take my seat. Today we are going to be assigned our groups for a class project. I have been dreading this all week. The longer the teacher puts off assigning us to our groups, the more anxious I feel. What if I get stuck with the kid who goofs off all the time? What if no one in the group likes my ideas?

Finally! The teacher pairs me with a kid. Oh, no! *Panic!* What's the kid's name? I have known this kid since kindergarten. *Think!* I thought elephants were supposed to have a good memory, or something. Not my ADHD elephant!

"Yes!" saved by the bell.

Class is over, and I don't have to worry about Mr. What's-his-name until tomorrow.

After school, I meet up with a friend. We have been friends since first grade and get along well since we both like computers and technology. I am happy being part of my own crowd instead of part of the "in crowd".

* * *

Did you know?

International Friendship Day is celebrated each year on July 30th. There is "chemistry" between you and your friends. Your genes (not the jeans you wear) are passed on to you from your parents and determine what you look like and who you are. In addition to your family members, your friends have some of the same genes as you.

7

"To invent, you need a good imagination and a pile of junk."

Thomas Edison

My ADHD Brain Is a Black Hole of Creativity

Black holes are areas of outer space with gravity so strong things get sucked in and never escape. My ADHD brain is like a black hole of creative ideas. I don't mind school projects, figuring out what I am going to do and how I am going to do it. The ADHD elephant can focus so much better on a crafty school project than on writing an essay for English class.

This week, I have to make a model of a bacteria cell for science class.

"Mom, can we go to the craft store? I need supplies for a school project."

Once there, I jump out of the car and run into the craft store. Mom can barely keep up. I zip in and out of the aisles, looking for supplies; a constant stream of ideas swirling around in my tornado brain.

As soon as we get home, I race upstairs to work on my model, eager to get started. As I work on my project, I suddenly I get a whiff of the delicious cookies Mom is baking. I can't wait to eat them with the ice cream she bought at the store yesterday. I emerge from my room, go downstairs, and find Mom and Dad in the kitchen.

"Andrew!"

Mom probably won't let me have any cookies now, it's too close to dinner.

"Andrew, what's that in your hands?"

Oh, right, my cell model. "It's the model I made of a bacteria cell for science class."

Mom and Dad both look at the model and remark on my originality and creativity. Mom and Dad are always telling me how creative, imaginative, and good at solving problems I am. The next day at school when I turn in my cell model, the science teacher likes it so much she displays it in her classroom. My black hole ADHD brain made me do it but in a good way this time.

When I get home from school the next day, I head up to my room and grab the paper airplane book off my desk. Flipping through the book, I try to decide which model to make. Out of the corner of my eye, I see the pile of clothes on my bedroom floor. Mom asked me to clean those up. Oh, well!

Book in hand, I walk downstairs and into the dining room after grabbing Mom's scissors from the kitchen, the ones she is always looking for because I constantly lay them down in random places. I get to work cutting out the parts of the airplane model. Where did I leave the glue? Scanning the table piled with abandoned craft projects, half-finished paper airplanes, broken electronics, model rockets, and empty paint bottles, I spot the glue on its side with the cap off. Glop plop. A big ball of glue oozes out of the tube and all over my thumb as I start gluing the paper airplane together. My thoughts drift aimlessly as I stare out of the window in the dining room. It's a sunny day. Maybe I will ask Dad if he wants to throw the football outside, or maybe I can ride my bike to my friend's house.

Oh, no! Looking back to my paper airplane, I realize my thumb is stuck to Mom's dining room table. I pry it off only to see an incriminating glue thumb print left behind. I grab some random papers from the graveyard of unfinished craft projects on the table and cover the glue thumbprint, hoping Mom won't notice. Not likely.

Heading outside to ride my bike, I spot the jar of craft sticks sitting on the worktable in the garage. That jar is always turning up in random places! Forgetting about everything else, I jump on my bike, pedal faster and faster, and speed down the driveway and onward to my friend's house.

* * *

Did you know?

Having a creative, imaginative, problem-solving ADHD brain can make you better at music, art, or computer games. I play the piano and the trumpet although my ADHD brain doesn't like to practice since practicing is boring. I like to make objects out of paper, using a folding technique called origami, and I take pottery lessons. David Neeleman, who started the successful JetBlue airline company, says his ADHD brain is what makes him successful since he is able to be creative and "think outside the box."

Kristin M. Wilcox, Ph.D. with Andrew S. Wilcox

8

"Never do anything by halves if you want to get away with it. Be outrageous. Make sure everything you do is so completely crazy it's unbelievable."

Author Roald Dahl

<u>A</u>dventurous, <u>D</u>aring, and Plunging <u>H</u>eadfirst into a <u>D</u>ilemma (ADHD or Superhero?)

A bowl of popcorn on my lap and remote in hand, I settle in on the couch to watch one of my favorite superhero movies. Who wouldn't want to be a superhero? They are courageous in the face of danger, have awesome superpowers, get to be adventurous, and are good looking.

However, my ADHD brain doesn't like to pay attention very long. So, I get bored with the movie and go outside to ride bikes with my brother in the driveway.

My brother and I decide it will be fun to tie one end of a piece of rope we found in the garage onto the back of my bike and the other end onto a shelf in our garage to see what would happen when I rode the bike out of the garage and into the driveway. *Crash!* Basketballs, baseball mitts, tennis rackets, fishing poles, golf balls, and miscellaneous sports equipment fly off the shelf and scatter all over the garage floor. Seeing a basketball bouncing out of the garage and heading towards Mom's car, I jump off my bike and chase the ball, hoping to catch it in time.

When I hear the door from the garage to the house being flung open, I stop dead in my tracks. Uh, oh! I'm in trouble!

Walking back toward the garage, basketball in hand, I hear my older brother frantically trying to explain to Mom how I simply bumped into the shelf by accident while riding my bike and it fell over. Mom just stands there, arms crossed, eyes narrowed, staring directly at me. Is that steam coming out of her ears? I can tell she is definitely *not* buying my brother's story.

"How did Andrew manage to make it out of the garage without the shelf falling on him?" she asks.

"I am invincible, just like a superhero," I tell her.

Mom is standing perfectly still in the doorway, looking like a predator ready to pounce on its prey. Staring at the ground and being careful not to make eye contact with Mom, I tell her I'll clean up the garage. How come in the movies superheroes never have to clean up their path of destruction? I guess they never get caught by their moms.

When my brother and I finish cleaning up the garage, I walk into the house. Dad is sitting in the kitchen.

"Andrew, will you help me fix the computer?"

"Sure!"

Just like a superhero, the ADHD elephant and I love a good challenge. My mind starts racing with ideas about how to get the computer working. Sometimes, focusing is easier when I am faced with a challenge and need to solve a difficult problem. Dad and I have the computer working by dinnertime.

After dinner, Mom reminds me I still need to do my homework.

"I know; I'm going." Reluctantly.

I remember I have homework for English class. Once again, it's the night before the assignment is due. Why do I always wait until the last minute? Where's the instructions for the assignment? Ouch! Stupid Legos are still scattered all over my bedroom floor. One of these days I will get around to cleaning them up.

I walk over to my bed and grab my backpack from where I threw it when I came home from school today. Crumpled up in the bottom of my backpack is the paper with the instructions. I stare at the directions written on the paper. Oh, great! I have to write *another* fictional story. My brain hurts, and I feel that familiar ache when I have a writing assignment to do.

Blink, blink, blink. The cursor keeps time on the blank screen as thoughts rush through my brain like a run-away freight train. Oh, where to begin? There are just too many details to think about. My thoughts drift aimlessly as I glance at the shelves above my desk filled with countless books about the planets, the moon, and rockets. Then I spot a paper rocket ship I made, peeking out from under some papers on my desk. Shoving the papers aside, I pick it up. Space travel! I can write my essay about space travel! I know a lot about space travel. It's one of my favorite things to learn about. Suddenly, my brain doesn't ache anymore. Furiously, I begin to type, turning my dreaded writing assignment into something I am interested in! Before I know it, I have written several pages. Superhero powers activate. I am hyperfocused. I remember my ADHD counselor mentioning something called hyperfocus in one of our sessions.

"It's when your ADHD brain has intense focus on a project or activity you find interesting she explained. "Hyperfocus can even make you an expert at something."

So, my ADHD brain can pay attention. I realize my passion for learning about space travel made writing my essay easy. I am like the Flash, whose passion for chemistry resulted in his incredible speed, or Iron Man, whose knowledge of technology helps him fight villains. My ADHD makes me a superhero.

Contrary to the dread I usually feel, I can't wait for my English teacher to grade my essay. When the teacher finally hands it back at the end of the week, a brightly colored, glorious, red "A" and the words "Great job, Andrew!" adorn the top left corner of the page. I can barely contain my excitement.

A championship-winning college basketball coach named John Wooden used to tell his team, "Don't let what you can't do stop you from doing what you can do." It's good advice for someone like me, with ADHD. I have a creative, fearless, sometimes intensely focused ADHD brain that is an explosive tornado of disorganization. I will always have ADHD, but I am working on becoming more of <u>A</u> <u>D</u>etermined <u>H</u>yperfocused <u>D</u>reamer, and less <u>A</u>lways

Disorganized and Hopelessly Distracted. However, Mom isn't ready to put away her neon-colored sticky notes just yet.

* * *

Did you know?

There are many successful, famous people with ADHD. Here are just a few.

1. Olympic swimmer Michael Phelps is the most decorated Olympian of all time with 23 gold medals and 28 medals in all.

2. World champion and Olympic gymnast Simone Biles said her ADHD is nothing to be ashamed of and she is not afraid to let people know about it.

3. Professional football quarterback Terry Bradshaw is in the National Football League's Hall of Fame and has won the Superbowl four times.

4. Astronaut Scott Kelly holds the record for the most time in space by an American astronaut. He has been a Space Shuttle pilot and the commander of several Space Shuttle missions to the International Space Station.

5. Successful actress Emma Watson played Hermione Granger in the Harry Potter movies.

6. Singers Adam Levine of the group Maroon 5 and Justine Timberlake both have ADHD and popular songs on the radio.

7. Nobel Prize winning scientist John B. Gurdon is my favorite person with ADHD. When John was 15 years old, his biology teacher did not believe that John should become a scientist. The biology teacher wrote on John's report card that he had trouble listening in class, did not complete his work, and struggled to learn simple facts. In 2012, Dr. Gurdon won the Nobel Prize, the highest honor a scientist can receive for his research, in physics.

Kristin M. Wilcox, Ph.D. with Andrew S. Wilcox

PART II
Kristin's Story

Kristin M. Wilcox, Ph.D. with Andrew S. Wilcox

9

Let the Chaos Commence

"Why can't you just clean your room, start your homework, study for your test, and put your bike away?" I cannot count the number of times I have said the words "Why can't you just" to Andrew, my son, who has Attention Deficit Hyperactivity Disorder (ADHD). I thought I understood ADHD. I had a PhD and was an academic researcher with a background in Psychology and Neuroscience. I knew about the brain chemistry likely involved in ADHD, and I had studied ADHD medications. Even after all this, I still did not understand my ADHD son. It never occurred to me Andrew couldn't just get things done. It was not a question of him understanding what needed to be done or being defiant; Andrew has difficulty focusing on disliked and mundane tasks, like straightening up his room or doing his homework. I remember reading an article on ADHD in which the author equated completing a task with ADHD to writing cursive using your non-dominant hand while having one of your feet make circles, the other foot move side to side, and tapping your head with your dominant hand. Simply put, a task you or I may consider routine, kids with ADHD view as overwhelming and can struggle with daily.

Attention deficit hyperactivity disorder is a neurobiological disorder resulting from an imbalance of certain chemicals in the brain. It is one of the most common neurobiological disorders, occurring in approximately 4-7% of children in the United States. According to the National Center for Health Statistics 2017 brief, in 2012-2013 6.1 million physician office visits were ADHD related. Heredity plays an important part in ADHD. If a child has ADHD, there is a 10-35% chance an immediate family member also has the disorder, and if the relative is a parent, there is a 57% chance the child will have ADHD. Abnormal levels of a chemical in the brain called dopamine are thought to contribute to the symptoms of ADHD. Dopamine's action in the brain can affect attention and is involved in novelty seeking/risk taking behaviors. Brain imaging studies show dopamine-rich areas of the brain, like the frontal cortex, are affected in ADHD. In contrast, a diet high in sugary snacks and soda is not an underlying cause of ADHD, but a healthy diet may be beneficial in reducing the symptoms of ADHD. Additionally, bad parenting does not lead to a diagnosis of ADHD. However, parental behavior as the result of interacting with an ADHD child may increase ADHD symptoms. For example, a cycle of a child not being on task and getting bad grades, parents becoming frustrated, and then the child becoming frustrated can bring out symptoms of ADHD. When Andrew would forget to turn in assignments for school, I would get frustrated with him, he would yell at me, I would yell back at him, and then he would have a full-blown meltdown as a result of the emotional dysregulation that occurs in ADHD. After I understood why Andrew was not turning in assignments and why he had extreme emotional responses to frustrating situations, I realized I had to modify my behavior that was contributing to Andrew's emotional meltdowns.

Andrew was in 2nd grade when my husband and I began to discuss his problems in paying attention in school, his disorganization, and his forgetfulness with his teachers and our pediatrician. After a year of wait-and-see, we had Andrew officially evaluated for ADHD. There were questionnaires for my husband and me to fill out as well as Andrew's two teachers at the time. The scores on all four questionnaires indicated Andrew had ADHD, and upon further evaluation by the school psychologist, he was diagnosed with the inattentive subtype of ADHD. There are three different subtypes of ADHD:

- Hyperactive (primarily symptoms of impulsivity and hyperactivity);

- Inattentive (primarily symptoms of inattention and difficulty focusing); and

- Combined (several symptoms of impulsivity, hyperactivity, and inattention).

Interestingly, when I surveyed some moms and dads in our school district and asked them what came to mind when they specifically thought about a boy with ADHD, most of their responses included behaviors like "impulsive, can't sit still, energetic, fidgets." Although this was not a formal research study with hundreds of participants, it makes a point that when most people think about a boy with ADHD, they assume the boy has some sort of impulsive and hyperactive behaviors.

On the contrary, boys can have inattentive type ADHD, like Andrew, with minimal impulsivity and hyperactivity. According to the National Institute of Mental Health, symptoms of inattentive type ADHD are less likely to be diagnosed and treated. However, studies in children have shown the inattentive subtype of ADHD may be as common as the combined subtype.

The onset of inattentive type ADHD symptoms may not be evident until around ages 9-11. Until recently, the current diagnostic criteria for ADHD required symptoms be present in the child by age 7, leading to relatively few children with the inattentive subtype of ADHD being diagnosed and receiving treatment. In addition, research suggests there are neurobiological differences between the combined and inattentive presentations of ADHD which affect symptomology and response to medical treatment. My husband has a saying when the kids or I make assumptions about something: "All cars are blue because the one I saw was." His saying can sum up diagnosing ADHD: not all kids have the same set of symptoms, and just because your child isn't hyperactive doesn't mean he/she does not have ADHD.

Attention "Deficit" Disorder is actually a misnomer. Kids with ADHD can pay attention; they just happen to pay attention to everything. Since ADHD kids are paying attention to everything all the time, they have difficulty paying attention to and completing one specific task.

It seems to be a contradiction, but ADHD kids can hyperfocus, or have intense focus on something that they are interested in, almost to the point of obsession. For Andrew, it's his relentless learning about anything related to outer space. rocket ships, and space travel. All of Andrew's knowledge about outer space is self-taught from reading books and visiting various educational websites on the computer. Because of his interest and intense focus, Andrew was a national finalist in an essay contest about traveling to Mars. Hyperfocus can be a positive symptom of ADHD, enabling your child to become an expert at something, hopefully boosting his/her confidence despite daily struggles with the negative symptoms of ADHD.

I remember my dad talking to Andrew's older brother before he was going on a date with a girl for the first time in high school. He told my son it's all about perception, how the girl and her parents will view him, what they will think about him based on his actions and appearance. Perception plays an important part in our behavior. On a television show about perception and the human brain, the show's creators conducted an experiment to observe human behavior in response to a person who appeared injured and in need of assistance. When the subject was dressed in professional business attire, several people passing by stopped to help her. In contrast, when the same woman was dressed in torn, dirty clothes, people passing by never offered her help. The behavior of the passersby was based purely on the woman's appearance; shabby, torn clothes symbolized that she must not have a job and is a lower-class citizen. Maybe the woman has a successful landscaping business and wears those clothes because she is digging in the dirt all day. Having a child with ADHD forced me to change my perception of what I thought I knew about the disorder, which was the negative symptoms of inattention, daydreaming, hyperactivity and impulsivity. Although ADHD kids will face challenges due to their negative symptoms, some of those "problems" may also help them to be successful. For example, kids with ADHD are creative thinkers and can come up with unique solutions to a problem, something our non-ADHD brains may struggle with. A lot of human progress has been thanks to "outside the box" thinkers. In addition, some characteristics of ADHD, like hyperfocus and risk taking, are known characteristics of entrepreneurs.

This was Andrew's life, he would always have ADHD, so it was time to embrace the creative and unique way his mind works and help him navigate through the negative symptoms of his ADHD. Some days it is a monumental task to try to keep everything in perspective, especially when I am being tuned out to play a computer game, homework is not being turned in, and it looks like a bomb exploded in Andrew's bedroom.

10

ADHD Can Make It Difficult
to Show What You Know

Albert Einstein once said "Everyone is a genius, but if you judge a fish by its ability to climb a tree, it will live its whole life believing it is stupid." Too often, kids with ADHD are expected to act and perform in school like their neurotypical peers. Unfortunately, due to the stigma associated with being labeled as ADHD, your child may be thought of as having a lower intelligence and denied certain opportunities where he/she might excel. When Andrew was in elementary school, I suggested to his teachers he would be successful in the advanced classes offered in math and science. However, their view was not the same as mine. Andrew's teachers were concerned about him falling behind since he had a diagnosis of ADHD. Despite the concern of his teachers, in 4th and 5th grade Andrew was one of the top performing students in math and science in the entire grade, and he even won a national award for excellence in math. Contrary to math and science, English is Andrew's least favorite subject and the class in which he struggles the most to stay focused and complete his work. We can all relate to being less motivated to do something mundane or unenjoyable, like laundry or paying bills, but we are mindful of the consequences: no clean clothes to wear or the electricity being turned off. However, children with ADHD struggle to overcome their dislike for something, like homework or a certain subject in school, and aren't motivated by the potential consequences, like a failing grade. Children with ADHD live in the here and now and are not concerned with what happened in the past or what may happen in the future.

Unfortunately, children with ADHD become under-stimulated more easily than their non-ADHD counterparts, especially with easy, rote, or long assignments at school, which can affect assignment correctness and completion. Additionally, children with ADHD struggle with the demanding verbal skills in school but excel in the less emphasized spatial and artistic skills. It is important to point out a child, like Andrew, with inattentive type ADHD often understands the subject material required to complete an undesirable assignment and can get A's and B's when the work is completed. In fact, research on ADHD symptoms and academic performance suggest that inattention and intelligence are unrelated. Similarly, reading difficulties in ADHD children are not associated with intelligence, but rather the inattention symptoms of ADHD likely interfere with reading ability. Finally, some children with

ADHD are considered twice exceptional due to their intellectual giftedness combined with a diagnosis of ADHD. Adults with ADHD have been reported to have intelligence quotients (IQs) of 120 or above, placing them into the top nine percent of the population. The symptoms of ADHD sometimes make it difficult to "show what you know" which can affect how ADHD kids are viewed in terms of academic ability.

So, if our ADHD kids are intelligent, why is it so difficult for them to pay attention, complete assignments for school, or follow a set of instructions, especially if they understand what to do? It has to do with executive functioning and working memory.

Executive functioning is a neurological process that enables us to pay attention to what is most important at the time so we can perform the appropriate behaviors. Additionally, executive functioning is important for planning and initiating tasks, time management, organization, and emotional control.

See if this scenario sounds familiar. Your ADHD child is engrossed in some activity of his/her choosing, like a video game or building with Legos, you give him/her a 15-minute warning to get ready for soccer practice. When you check on your child 15 minutes later, you find he/she has not moved, and you are now going to be late to practice. Kids with ADHD have trouble stopping inappropriate behaviors (playing a computer game, building Legos) to focus on appropriate behaviors (getting ready for soccer practice) due to their deficits in executive functioning. Another key component to why your ADHD child may seem distracted and forgetful is working memory, our most immediate form of memory.

Working memory allows us to store information in our brains to be used later. Let's say you are solving a multistep math problem, for example 10+15-2=? You calculate 10+15=25, you can hold the number 25 in your memory stores due to working memory so you can go on to complete the rest of the problem, 25-2=23. Another example is when you are following a recipe, your working memory enables you to remember which ingredients you already added. Children with ADHD can forget what they were supposed to be paying attention to since the important information held in their working memory can easily be replaced by other stimuli like video games or building Legos.

As parents and caregivers, we have to learn how to work with a child's ADHD brain for that child to be successful. When Andrew comes home from school, he is not at all interested in doing homework or studying; he goes straight to the computer to play some game or to the dining room table to work on something crafty.

One night for homework, Andrew had to study for a test on a book he had just finished reading for English class. When he came home from school that day, Andrew went into the dining room to work on a paper airplane model. I decided to try an experiment with Andrew to get him to study for his test on the book. While Andrew was cutting out and gluing together pieces for his latest

paper airplane model, I started going over the study g
the teacher had given his class for the test. Andrew did
remarkably well. He remembered details of the book and
answered all the questions on the study guide correctly
without resistance or frustration. Children with ADHD
have better focus when they manipulate something with
their hands. Physically moving their hands to manipulate
something helps to increase attention by affecting the
levels of dopamine in certain brain areas.

Kristin M. Wilcox, Ph.D. with Andrew S. Wilcox

11

Some Days I Need to Seek Shelter
from the Tornado

I wouldn't characterize myself as a "neat freak" although my husband and children would say otherwise. Having a child with ADHD whose idea of organization is a big pile on the floor has been a bit of a challenge for me. Andrew loves to go to flea markets and shop for antiques, and his "treasures" always seem to end up thrown on a miscellaneous pile shoved into a corner on the floor of his bedroom.

One weekend I mentioned to Andrew we were going to clean out his room, which was getting too cluttered with all his collections. Andrew's response to me was "Mom, why are we bothering to clean up my room? It's going to stay organized for all of ten minutes. You know me; I'm not organized."

Although this made me chuckle, Andrew's statement was true. The struggle with organization for children with ADHD stems from their executive function deficits. Creating and maintaining an organizational system requires planning, initiating the task for knowing what needs to be organized, and finding a place for something based on how often it is used. These complex processes require working memory and are a challenge for an ADHD brain. When Andrew is supposed to be cleaning up his room, I usually find him surrounded by a bigger mess on his floor, playing with some treasure he misplaced a month ago.

I set out on the task of helping Andrew to become more organized and along the way found out that my organization techniques don't always work for an ADHD brain. I love my bins and baskets. Unfortunately, I am the only one in my family who feels this way. In fact, my husband rejoices every time I get rid of a basket. Andrew, on the other hand, is a throw-it-on- the-floor-table-or-countertop type of organizer. He also lives in a constant state of near-hording and never wants to get rid of anything, which presents another challenge to being organized. After several failed attempts to help Andrew be more organized, I realized I needed to enlist Andrew's help to find a solution that works for him and not one that works for me. For example, Andrew will never put something away in a bin and then put the bin on a shelf; that involves working memory. The bin will be left open on the floor for weeks. The contents of the bin will be emptied out on the floor and left there for the dog to chew on, or, if stacked on some shelf, the bin and its contents will be forgotten completely.

As Andrew progressed in school, there came a point, around 6th grade, when he had so many assignments to keep track of his grades began to suffer. I worried about Andrew missing out on opportunities because his grades were low and also worried his teachers may not know his capabilities. According to a 2016 report by the Centers for Disease Control and Prevention, 90% of students with ADHD receive classroom accommodations in school. However, most children with ADHD are not in special education programs, and their teachers may know little about ADHD behaviors.

Andrew and I argue at least once a week about his school folder, which is crammed with so many papers it is bursting at the seams and ripped in half. I am usually trying to get him to locate a missing assignment for school or instructions for a school project. After one such argument, I finally had had enough; it was time to contain Andrew's chaos. His disorganization was resulting in failing grades due to incomplete work that was being stuffed in the folder and forgotten. If Andrew couldn't keep track of his schoolwork in middle school, how was he ever going to survive the rigorous course load in high school? I knew Andrew was more capable than his grades reflected and had every intention of getting his work done, but his disorganized ADHD brain sometimes derailed him along the way. It was time to come up with a solution.

Children with ADHD immediately respond to every new stimulus around them, which leads to their attention shifting from something less desirable, like organizing a school folder, to a more enjoyable activity, like riding a bike outside on a sunny day. In order to help Andrew be more organized, we had to help his working memory. The less Andrew's working memory needs to work and remember on its own, the more successful he will be.

Ways to help working memory can include writing down reminders for what needs to be done, giving a to-do item a deadline by writing it on a calendar, breaking down a large task into several smaller ones, and setting a certain amount of time to focus on completing a task. Andrew and I came up with a plan for him to clean out his folder once a week on the same day. We have also used the same plan for cleaning up his crafting supplies and his bedroom. Since organizing the craft table and the bedroom are larger, and more overwhelming, tasks than cleaning out his school folder, we have added additional strategies to help Andrew complete these chores. Simply telling Andrew it's time to clean up is like telling someone who builds model rockets to go and build an actual rocket to get someone to Mars; they wouldn't know where to start, and the task would be very daunting. So, to break down the task for Andrew, I give him a very specific list of what needs to be done, for example:

1. Pick up your clothes from the floor and put them in the hamper.

2. Clean off the dresser.

3. Make the bed.

The list has a maximum of five items; otherwise, there are too many for him to complete. Andrew uses a timer and sets a duration of time for cleaning up, followed by a shorter duration of time for a break. During the break, Andrew can do an activity of his choosing. Setting a timer helps with time management, which is another struggle for children with ADHD, and is useful for other tasks, like completing homework assignments. Of course, there is no guarantee the homework will be turned in on time and not end up in the abyss of papers in a folder that is ready to explode.

I have learned it takes a monumental amount of patience, an open mind, and a lot of trial and error to find strategies to help Andrew's ADHD brain to be organized. Typical of ADHD kids, a strategy may work for a while, then become boring when the novelty of the new strategy wears off. However, a flutter of excitement goes through me every time I find Andrew has put his socks in the hamper, and I try not to notice the pile of underwear on the floor.

Kristin M. Wilcox, Ph.D. with Andrew S. Wilcox

12

ADHD and the Incredible Hulk

Andrew loves to build Legos sets. When Andrew was younger, it was inevitable he would eventually get to a point where he couldn't find a certain piece in the sea of Lego pieces scattered on the floor and then would have a meltdown. He would argue, loudly, with my husband that the piece was missing from the set. It was no use pointing out to Andrew he had said this about previous Lego sets he built, which were all complete with no missing pieces. Although Andrew's behavior may seem like an overreaction, kids with ADHD often get frustrated quickly, make something way more important than it really is, have trouble calming down once they are angry, and are often offensive when criticized. My husband often tells Andrew building Legos should be fun and suggests Andrew take a break when he is upset about not being able to find the piece he needs. Sometimes stepping away from a task or frustrating situation helps Andrew have a better perspective; this takes an enormous amount of practice, even for someone without ADHD.

Unfortunately, emotional dysregulation is one of the negative symptoms of ADHD. Anger and frustration are regulated through executive functioning. Additionally, deficits in working memory interfere with learning from previous experiences. Therefore, kids with ADHD have more difficulty managing their emotions compared to their peers and often react to a frustrating situation in an impulsive and explosive manner instead of responding to it. Our household was not immune to sibling rivalry when the boys were younger. Andrew had difficulty ignoring his older brother when he would taunt him and call him names. The result was Andrew screaming and yelling at his brother at the top of his lungs, red-faced, and completely out of breath. The yelling was usually followed by stomping into his bedroom and slamming his door so hard the items on his shelves would fall off. Andrew is aware of his behavior, and it is not something he likes about himself.

One afternoon, I picked Andrew up from the bus stop when he was in middle school, and when he got in the car, I could see he was crying. When I asked Andrew what happened, he told me about an incident on the bus with three older girls who were making fun of him. One of the girls took pictures of him with her smartphone while he was getting upset. Andrew, in an impulsive, explosive reaction to the situation, knocked the girl's phone out of her hands and yelled back at his tormenters. Andrew was immediately embarrassed by his behavior since he never had an outburst of anger in public before.

As his parent, it is difficult to watch Andrew lose control of his emotions. When Andrew is in a full-blown tantrum, I try to remember he is not making the choice to act in such an explosive manner. I also need to keep my temper in check to avoid a screaming match with no resolution to what aggravated Andrew in the first place. Unlike other kids, those with ADHD have trouble realizing that what is frustrating them may not be such a big deal after all.

Andrew began seeing a therapist several years ago because my husband and I were concerned about his emotional outbursts. At the time, we did not realize his emotional outbursts were part of his ADHD. In fact, the currently accepted diagnostic criteria for an ADHD diagnosis does not include lack of emotional control; however, research shows that low tolerance of frustration, hot temper, and impatience are all part of ADHD. Acknowledging that it was okay for him to get angry was important for Andrew as was making sure he knew even kids without ADHD get angry. Once Andrew's emotions start to get the best of him, I've learned the hard way, it is better to let him walk away instead of following him and trying to get the last word in. When he has calmed down and has his emotions in check, he is ready to dive back into a project and will even apologize for his behavior.

Kids with ADHD live in the here and now, often getting caught up in their emotions. In addition to executive function deficits, mindset may play a role in emotional dysregulation. Carol Dweck, a psychologist at

Stanford University, has proposed two types of mindsets: a fixed mindset, and a growth mindset.

According to Dweck's research, individuals with a fixed mindset believe they have a certain set of skills and those skills cannot be modified or changed; you are good at something or you are not. Those with a fixed mindset are afraid of failure and feel if they are not very good at something there is no need to work at it. In contrast, individuals with a growth mindset view mistakes as learning opportunities to help them perform better in the future.

Children and adults with ADHD often have a fixed mindset and feel frustrated when they struggle to complete a task, they believe they are not good at. For example, I see the fixed mindset in Andrew when he is building one of his model airplanes and struggles to get some of the tiny pieces to stay together. I have often heard the words, "I am not good at this," as he becomes increasingly frustrated with something he is trying to do. The good news is someone can change from having a fixed mindset to having a growth mindset. According to Dweck, the key is to praise your child's effort. For example, if your child receives an A on a test say you are proud of him because of the effort he put into studying for the test instead of telling him how smart he is. When Andrew is becoming frustrated while building his model, I try to point out to him how much he has already accomplished.

13

Good Ol' Whatshisname?

It used to concern me that Andrew could not name half of the kids in his grade, most of whom he has been in school with since kindergarten. I often remind Andrew to ask someone his/her name if he does not know it. It seemed simple enough, but then Andrew's ADHD brain kicked in. Attention and working memory are two key components of cognitive functioning which allows us to, among other things, put a name to a face. When it comes to remembering someone's name, we can all relate to having an ADHD brain. Have you ever been in a situation where you wanted to introduce a friend to someone you see frequently at school functions but just can't seem to remember her/his name? Our cognitive functions decline with age, making our brains more ADHD-like, and suddenly we find ourselves struggling to put a name to a face. So, for someone like Andrew, with ADHD, it's hard to make friends in school, especially if you can't remember the name of the kid you want to talk to.

Kids with ADHD are often viewed negatively by their peers due to their symptoms of inattention, immaturity, hyperactivity, impulsivity, poor emotional control, and aggression. A study in elementary school children revealed the detrimental effect of an ADHD label. In the study, children expected to have ADHD, whether they had it or not, were viewed in a more negative manner by peers than children not labeled as ADHD. ADHD kids have little self-awareness: they don't pay attention to their emotions, feelings, behaviors, and how they affect others. As a result, kids with ADHD can often appear callous, uncaring, or socially inept. Negative attitudes by peers are difficult to dispel over time, and approximately one third of teens and adults with ADHD are fearful of being seen by others as incompetent, unappealing, or uncool. I recall Andrew saying to me when he was in eighth grade that he was not included in an online chat group created by one of the kids in his class because he was the "weird kid." In addition, a lack of self-awareness can lead to ADHD kids feeling misunderstood and under-appreciated. When Andrew has a group project for school, he will often report to me no one in the group wants to listen to his ideas, and he feels like his opinion is not valued. Developing meaningful peer relationships can be a challenge for kids with ADHD due to the negative symptoms of their ADHD and their lack of self-awareness.

Most people associate with peers who have similar interests to their own. I have come to believe this is especially important for Andrew and other kids with ADHD who struggle socially. The summer after seventh grade Andrew attended a week-long space camp where he got to train like an astronaut. Although he didn't know any one and the camp was over 14 hours away, he was more excited for the camp than for anything he had done before. During camp, whenever I talked to Andrew on the phone, he was always having a wonderful time with his new friends. This seems atypical for an ADHD kid who has difficulty with social interaction. However, just like Andrew, all the kids at the camp were passionate about space travel, rocket building, and learning about outer space. Andrew's ADHD didn't matter; at the camp he wasn't the "weird kid." Having something in common with the kids at camp helped Andrew to form lasting peer relationships, and he keeps in touch with the kids whom he met there. Andrew's space camp experience was featured on our county's school website giving him the opportunity to be the "cool kid" and boost his self-esteem.

In addition to his passion for learning about outer space, Andrew has always been interested in music; he plays both the trumpet and the piano. Kids with ADHD are often gifted when it comes to music, thanks to their creative minds. When he started high school, I convinced Andrew he should join the school's marching band. Although Andrew was reluctant at first, it turned out to be a wonderful experience for him, one he thoroughly enjoys. Once again, he was surrounded by kids with a common interest. He suddenly had a group of friends to hang out with before school, eat lunch with, and get together with outside of school. Finally, Andrew felt like he belonged, and although, he will probably never be part of the "in crowd," he will be part of his own crowd.

14

My Life with a Crafty Stuntman

Noted Harvard psychiatrist and author of the international best seller *Driven to Distraction: Recognizing and Coping with Attention Deficit Disorder*, Dr. Edward (Ned) Hallowell believes ADHD can be a gift. He focuses on a strength-based approach when treating his ADHD patients, helping them to realize there is more to ADHD than the negative symptoms, they are also intelligent, creative, imaginative and risk-takers.

When Andrew was in middle school my husband and I decided to relinquish our dining room table to Andrew's creativity and craftiness. I just wanted scraps of paper, bottles of glue, and model rocket kits in various stages of completion off the kitchen table, the family room floor, the piano, or any other flat surface Andrew could find to craft on. I love Andrew's creative mind; it's something positive about his ADHD. Creativity is often defined as original, outside-the-box thinking, and the ability to combine unrelated ideas for a unique solution to a problem. Like many ADHD children, Andrew's brain is constantly being bombarded with information, and his brain cannot sort through what is relevant and what is not due to deficits in executive functioning. An ADHD child's creativity is a result of the brain not filtering out the irrelevant incoming information. It is their diffuse attention that leads to original and imaginative problem-solving abilities.

Research studies suggest children with ADHD may be better at music, art, and computers. Additionally, they may be more inquisitive about how things work and have imaginative ideas about how to solve a problem. However, the attention getter for kids with ADHD may be the challenge of finding a solution, rather than following through to completion. When asked to create a new unique toy, children with ADHD were better at generating ideas compared to their non-ADHD peers who were better at developing the idea further. Andrew takes pottery lessons and would much rather put his attention into thinking of and creating a piece on the pottery wheel than glazing, or painting, it. I often get "Mom, you can finish glazing that" because he doesn't find that part of making a completed pottery piece as challenging, and therefore it doesn't hold his attention for very long.

Independence, risk-taking, high energy, curiosity, humor, artistic gifts, emotionality, impulsiveness, argumentativeness, and hyperactivity are traits that have been identified in creative individuals, entrepreneurs, and children with ADHD. Creativity has been found to be important in successful job performance, healthy relationships, and careers involving science, technology, engineering, mathematics and art. According to Dr. Russell Barkley, a clinical psychologist and ADHD expert, 35% of people with ADHD are self-employed by their thirties, which is a higher percentage compared the population as a whole.

David Neeleman started the successful airline company JetBlue. Neeleman has said his ADHD is what makes him successful since he is able to be creative and think outside the box. Another highly successful entrepreneur with ADHD is Sir Richard Branson who started Virgin Records in the 1970's, then went on to build the Virgin Atlantic airline company, and his most recent company, Virgin Galactic, will take tourists into space. Branson's companies are in more than 30 countries and worth over $5 billion. Branson views his dyslexia and ADHD as strengths, not weaknesses. Andrew started a jewelry business using his talent at origami (the Japanese art of paper folding); he sells his jewelry at a local store in our hometown.

Risk-taking behavior is a defining symptom of ADHD. Children with ADHD truly are "Adrenaline Junkies." Getting their adrenaline pumping can be critical for maintaining attention and performance in children with ADHD. They can often play video games for hours due to the fast-paced action and dangerous situations present in the games. Similarly, some adults with ADHD report they can focus better when driving if they are speeding (although I am not recommending this!). When Andrew was in middle school, my introduction to the new principal was a call to inform me Andrew was no longer allowed to use his smartphone at school since he was trying to bypass a firewall intended to block student access to various Internet sites. For obvious reasons, the school restricts access to many Internet sites, and the site Andrew was attempting to access was one he frequently spends time on at home. Andrew's actions were not intended to be malicious, but the challenge and risk he might get caught were fueling his behavior. For an equally challenging but less risky endeavor Andrew enjoys fixing broken computers. He will spend hours taking the computers apart, figuring out why they don't work, fixing, and putting them back together again. I admire Andrew's willingness to take a chance, rise to a challenge, and be fearless. When Andrew went to space camp, he had the opportunity to go into a machine that simulated a space craft tumbling out of control, spinning you left, right and upside down. Of course, Andrew was first in line.

15

Rein in the Negative
Symptoms of ADHD

When Andrew was in second grade and his teacher suggested he was exhibiting symptoms of ADHD, I was not ready to jump right into a diagnosis and medicate him. Attention deficit hyperactivity disorder is diagnosed 2-4 times more often in boys than in girls, which may be due to referral patterns from teachers. In 2010, the Center for Disease Control and Prevention estimated two-thirds of children are medicated for the treatment of ADHD. The primary medications used to treat the symptoms of ADHD are from a group of drugs known as stimulants. Approximately three million children in the United States take stimulant medications to help them focus, and roughly 60% of children with ADHD are treated with stimulants. Stimulant medications are thought to alleviate the negative symptoms of ADHD primarily though regulating the brain neurochemicals, norepinephrine and dopamine, which are decreased in certain brain regions. For Andrew, treatment with stimulant medication lead to improved focus at school, improved handwriting, and less disappearing to the bathroom during school time to avoid doing classwork. Although stimulant treatment can improve attention and focus, it will not affect the ability to learn or to apply learned concepts in a child with ADHD. Andrew has even said to me that taking his medication will not make him an A student, that he still needs to put in the effort to get good grades in school. Interestingly, someone with ADHD may not realize the benefit of medication due to his/her lack of self-awareness; adolescents with ADHD often ask to be taken off medication because they do not perceive it is helping them. After his first semester in high school, Andrew asked if he had to continue taking his medication. We decided to let him come off his medication; however, I stay in contact with Andrew's teachers to ensure he is staying focused and on task in school.

Prescription stimulants, such as those used to treat ADHD, may be misused by individuals with and without ADHD. The nonmedical use of prescription stimulants by college students is second only to marijuana use. College students typically use prescription stimulants to improve focus and concentration or to induce euphoria (get "high"). Initially, I did not want Andrew to be on medication when he started high school and have "friends" because he was on ADHD medication. Unfortunately, studies have shown students taking prescription medications for ADHD treatment are solicited by peers to give, sell, or trade their medications, even as early as elementary school. Several studies over the years have addressed potential concerns (e.g.: growth deficits and future substance abuse disorder) of long-term treatment with stimulant medications. Currently, there is no definitive evidence to suggest detrimental effects of continuous stimulant exposure for the treatment of ADHD. In fact, research suggests substance abuse disorder in ADHD individuals is likely related to their ADHD (risk-taking behavior) and not to treatment with stimulant medications.

According to the National Institute of Mental Health's 2009 Multimodal Treatment Study of Children with ADHD, the most successful treatments for ADHD include medication and behavioral therapy. Over the years, Andrew has developed behaviors and habits that contribute to his inattentiveness, disorganization, and emotional dysregulation. We can all relate to the difficulty of trying to break one habit in favor of a more beneficial behavior. For instance, not eating dessert every night after dinner or taking the stairs at work instead of the elevator if you are trying to maintain a healthy lifestyle. For a child struggling with the symptoms of ADHD, changing an undesired behavior is even more of a challenge. Additionally, a child with ADHD will often have difficulty consistently applying a modified behavior. Finally, it takes a lot of trial and error along with patience on the part of the parent to find something that works. Andrew meets with both a psychologist and an executive function coach to help him modify his negative ADHD symptoms. One of the biggest struggles for Andrew is remembering to write down homework or project assignments for school.

As Andrew progressed in school, the list of dates and assignments became longer, and his working memory deficits were interfering with him being able to remember the numerous assignments he had every day. As a result, many assignments and projects were incomplete, and Andrew's grades began to fall. We have gone through countless strategies to try to get Andrew to write down school assignments: different types of planners, pop-up reminders on his smartphone, a white board calendar, and a neon-colored assignment sheet in his school folder, just to name a few.

In addition to medication and behavioral therapy, regular exercise can improve focus in children with ADHD, according to Dr. John Ratey, Associate Clinical Professor of Psychiatry at Harvard Medical School. Exercise increases levels of the brain chemicals, dopamine and norepinephrine, helping to alleviate the inattention associated with ADHD. Exercise can also help regulate emotional control and fidgetiness. More complicated exercises such as martial arts, gymnastics, mountain biking, rock climbing, and skateboarding have the greatest effect on improving focus and concentration. According to Dr. Ratey, these types of exercises put the brain on high alert for the fight-or-flight response. In other words, there is motivation to learn the skills for these technical and challenging activities so you don't get hit by your opponent in karate, fall of your bicycle while riding on dangerous terrain, or tumble when climbing a rock face. Some activities that appeal to Andrew are indoor rock climbing, martial arts, track and field, and high school marching band. Although marching band is not considered a traditional sport, the members of the band are required to do some minimal exercising to be able to hold up their instruments and move around on the field during performances. I believe it is the complicated choreography that appeals to Andrew; the constant movement, knowing where to be on the field, and what notes you should be playing at any given time.

Andrew gravitates towards individual, not team, sports. According to Dr. Patricia Quinn, a developmental pediatrician specializing in ADHD at the Pediatric Development Center in Washington DC., team sports like basketball and football which require the participants to know where players are on the field, anticipate player movements, and strategize are not ideal for children with ADHD. When Andrew was in elementary and middle school, he played basketball. Despite playing for a few years he never learned where to be on the court, never knew if he was on offense or defense, and never seemed to be able to make a basket. Finally, in seventh grade, Andrew decided basketball was no longer for him.

Kristin M. Wilcox, Ph.D. with Andrew S. Wilcox

Epilogue

There are undeniable negative symptoms of ADHD like disorganization, inattention, emotional dysregulation, and risk-taking behaviors, but there are also positive attributes of ADHD which can be nurtured, like creativity, intelligence, and challenge-seeking behaviors. Raising a successful child with ADHD is no small task. One of my most important roles is to be Andrew's advocate and to teach him to advocate for himself. The symptoms of inattentive-type ADHD only affect the individual. It is difficult for neurotypicals to understand the cognitive dysfunction associated with ADHD: missed deadlines are not due to laziness or apathy, but to disorganization and working memory deficits; and being late is not a purposeful disregard for another but the result of poor time management. Children with ADHD do not choose to fail classes in school, be disorganized, or have uncontrollable emotional outbursts. I myself have been guilty of forgetting this. I am learning to embrace my creative, risk-taking, emotional whirlwind of disorganization child and rise to the challenge of helping Andrew to be a success.

Kristin M. Wilcox, Ph.D. with Andrew S. Wilcox

Appendix A

Inattentive ADHD Symptoms: Are you like Andrew?

Difficulty focusing and easily distracted

- Do you have difficulty focusing on tasks you don't like, or want, to do like writing an essay for English class?

- Maybe you frequently visit the nurse or the bathroom during school when there is an assignment you don't want to complete.

- Do you rush through school assignments or turn in assignments that are incomplete?

- Do you wait until the last minute to start assignments for school, or chores?

- Do you play video games or look through a paper airplane book instead of doing homework or chores?

- Is your dining room table a graveyard of unfinished craft projects?

Difficulty paying attention and listening

- Do you often need to ask the teacher to repeat instructions for school assignments or homework?

- Do you walk around or look at your smartphone when Mom or Dad are trying to have a conversation with you?

Difficulty organizing and keeping track of stuff

- Is your backpack or desk a mess with crumpled papers stuffed everywhere?
- Do you set things down in random places and forget where they are, like your mom's scissors or the jar of craft sticks?

Difficulty remembering daily activities

- Do you need to be reminded to brush your teeth, or take your ADHD medication daily?
- Does your mom have to remind you to turn in homework, bring your trumpet home from school or clean your room on neon-colored sticky notes?

Difficulty controlling your emotions

- Do you get easily frustrated and have elephant-sized meltdowns?
- Do you get angry or cry more than you should, or when an adult tells you a situation isn't as bad as you think it is?

Creative

- Are you an outside-the-box thinker, making associations between two seemingly unrelated ideas?

- Do you excel at music, art, or crafty school projects?
- Do you enjoy hands-on projects?

Superhero

- Are you a good problem solver who enjoys a challenge?
- Are you fearless, jumping right in to the unknown?
- Are you an expert at something, like space travel, due to your hyperfocus superpower?

For more comprehensive information about inattentive ADHD symptoms, visit the American Psychiatric Association (www.psychiatry.org/patients-families/adhd/what-is-adhd) and the Centers for Disease Control and Prevention (www.cdc.gov/ncbddd/adhd/diagnosis) online.

Kristin M. Wilcox, Ph.D. with Andrew S. Wilcox

Appendix B

Additional ADHD Resources

ADHD Organizations

A.D.D. Resource Center: www.addrc.org, 646-205-8080

American Academy of Child and Adolescent Psychiatry: www.aacap.org, 202-966-7300

American Psychological Association: www.apa.org, 800-374-2721

Attention Deficit Disorder Association: www.add.org, 800-939-1019

Children and Adults with Attention Deficit Disorder (CHADD): www.chadd.org, 301-306-7070

Child Mind Institute: www.childmind.org, 212-308-3118

Inattentive ADHD Coalition: www.iadhd.org

Learning Disability Association of America: www. ldaamerica.org, 412-341-1515

Understood: www.understood.org

Books for ADHD Children

Marvin's Monster Diary: ADHD Attacks! (But I Rock It, Big Time) by Raun Melmed, M.D. and Annette Sexton (Familius, 2016).

The Survival Guide for Kids with ADHD by John F. Taylor, Ph.D. (Free Spirit Publishing, 2nd edition, 2013).

Journal of an ADHD Kid: The Good, the Bad, and the Useful by Tobias Stumpf and Dawn Schaefer Stumpf (Woodbine House, 2014).

Learning Outside the Lines by Jonathan Mooney and David Cole (Touchstone, 2000).

SOAR Study Skills by Susan Kruger, M.Ed. (Grand Lighthouse Publishers, 2017).

Books for Parents and Caregivers

What Your ADHD Child Wishes You Knew: Working Together to Empower Kids for Success in School and Life by Sharon Saline, Psy.D. (TarcherPerigee, 2018).

Parenting ADHD Now!: Easy Intervention Strategies to Empower Kids with ADHD by Elaine Taylor-Klaus and Diane Dempster (Althea Press, 2016).

Taking Charge of ADHD, Third Edition: The Complete, Authoritative Guide for Parents by Russell A. Barkley, Ph.D. (Guilford Press; 3rd edition, 2013).

Boy Without Instructions: Surviving the Learning Curve of Parenting a Child with ADHD by Penny Williams (Grace-Everett Press, 2014).

Superparenting for ADD: An Innovative Approach to Raising Your Distracted Child by Edward Hallowell, MD. and Peter Jenson (Ballantine 2008).

Periodicals

ADDitude Magazine: www.additudemag.com, 888-762-8475

Attention Magazine: www.chadd.org/get-attention-magazine/

Kristin M. Wilcox, Ph.D. with Andrew S. Wilcox

References

Albert, M., Rui, P., & Ashman, J.J. (2017). *Physician office visits for attention-deficit/hyperactivity disorder in children and adolescents Aged 4–17 Years: United States, 2012–2013.* National Center for Health Statistics. https://www.cdc.gov/nchs/products/databriefs/db269.htm.

Ansburg, P.I., & Hill, K. (2003). Creative and analytic thinkers differ in their use of attentional resources. *Personality and Individual Differences* 34: 1141-1152.

Applegate, B., Lahey, B.B., Hart, E.L., Biederman, J., Hynd, G.W., Barkley, R.A., Ollendick, T., Frick, P.J., Greenhill, L., McBurnett, K., Newcorn, J.H., Kerdyk, L., Garfinkel, B., Waldman, I., & Shaffer, D. (1997). Validity of the age-of-onset criterion for ADHD: A report from the DSM-IV field trials. *Journal of the American Academy of Child and Adolescent Psychiatry* 36: 1211-1221.

Brown, T.E. (n.d.). *Exaggerated emotions: How and why ADHD triggers intense feelings. Retrieved from https://www.additudemag.com/slideshows/adhd-emotions-understanding-intense-feelings* December 6, 2021.

Brown, T.E., Reichel, P.C., & Quinlan, D.M. (2009). Executive function impairments in high IQ adults with ADHD. *Journal of Attention Disorders*, 13(2), 161-167.

Carlson, C. L., & Mann, M. (2000). Attention-deficit hyperactivity disorder, predominantly inattentive subtype. *Child and Adolescent Psychiatric Clinics of North America* 9: 499-510.

Danielson, M.L., Bitsko, R.H., Ghandour, R.M., Holbrook, J.R., Kogan, M.D., & Blumberg, S.J. (2018). Prevalence of parent-reported ADHD diagnosis and associated treatment among U.S. children and adolescents, 2016. *Journal of Clinical Child and Adolescent Psychology* 47 (2): 199-212.

Diamond, A. (2005). Attention-deficit disorder (attention-deficit/hyperactivity disorder without hyperactivity): A neurobiologically and behaviorally distinct disorder from attention-deficit/hyperactivity disorder (with hyperactivity). *Developmental Psychopathology* 17(3): 807–825.

Dodson, W. (2020, September 30). *Uncomfortable truths about the ADHD nervous system.* ADDitude. https://www.additudemag.com/adhd-in-adults-nervous-system.

Dweck, Carol S. (2016) *Mindset: The new psychology of success.* New York: Random House.

Fritz, K.M., & O'Connor, P.J. (2016). Acute exercise improves mood and motivation in young men with ADHD symptoms. *Medicine & Science in Sports & Exercise* 48(6), 1153-1160.

Fugate, C.M., Zentall, S.S., & Gentry, M. (2013). Creativity and working memory in gifted students with and without characteristics of attention deficit hyperactive disorder: Lifting the mask. *Gifted Child Quarterly* 57: 234-246.

Gaub, M., & Carlson, C. L. (1997). Gender differences in ADHD: A meta-analysis and critical review. *Journal of the American Academy of Child and Adolescent Psychiatry* 36: 1035-1045.

Gilman, L. (2018, October 19). *How to succeed in business with ADHD.* ADDitude. https://www.additudemag.com/adhd-entrepreneur-stories-jetblue-kinkos-jupitermedia.

Hallowell, E.M., & Ratey, J.J. (2011) *Driven to distraction: Recognizing and coping with attention deficit disorder* (Rev. ed.). Prescott, AZ: Anchor.

Hendricks, L., Bore, S., Aslinia, D., & Morriss, G. (2013). The effects of anger on the brain and body. *National Forum Journal of Counseling and Addiction* 2(1): 1-12.

Hoza, B. (2007). Peer functioning in children with ADHD. *Ambulatory Pediatrics*, 7(1 Suppl):101–106.

Jacobson, R. (n.d.). *ADHD and exercise.* Child Mind Institute. https://www.childmind.org/ article/adhd-and-exercise.

Lakhan, S.E., & Kirchgessner, A. (2012). Prescription stimulants in individuals with and without attention deficit hyperactivity disorder: Misuse, cognitive impact, and adverse effects *Brain and Behavior* 2(5): 661–677.

Lara, M. (2012, June). The exercise prescription for ADHD. *Attention*, 19 (3): 22-24.

Maedgen, J. W., & Carlson, C. L. (2000). Social functioning and emotional regulation in the attention deficit hyperactivity disorder subtypes. *Journal of Clinical Child Psychology* 29: 30-42.

Matthews, M., Nigg, J.T., & Fair, D.A. (2014). Attention deficit hyperactivity disorder. *Current Topics in Behavioral Neuroscience* 16: 235–266.

Paloyelis, Y., Rijsdijk, F., Wood, A.C., Asherson, P., & Kuntsi, J. (2010). The genetic association between ADHD symptoms and reading difficulties: The role of inattentiveness and IQ. *Journal of Abnormal Child Psychology* 38: 1083–1095.

Ratey, J.J., & Hagerman, E. (2013). *Spark: The revolutionary new science of exercise and the brain.* Little, Brown.

Rodgers, A., & Kalyn, W. (2020, May 27). *The magic of individual sports.* ADDitude. https://www.additudemag.com/benefits-of-individual-sports.

Shoot, B. (2020, May 13). *The stars who aligned ADHD with success.* ADDitude. https://www.additudemag.com/ successful-people-with-adhd-learning-disabilities.

Singh, A., Yeh, C., Verma, N., & Das, A. (2015). Overview of Attention Deficit Hyperactivity Disorder in Young Children. *Health Psychology Research* 3(2): 23-35.

Solanto, M.V. (2001). Clinical grand rounds. Special issue on predominantly inattentive AD/HD. *The AD/HD Report* 9 (1): 12-15.

Solanto, M.V. (2000). The predominantly inattentive subtype of AD/HD. *CNS Spectrums* 5: 45-51.

Soto P.L., Wilcox, K.M., Zhou, Y., Ator, N.A., Riddle, M.A., Wong, D.F., & Weed, M.R. (2012). Long-term exposure to oral methylphenidate or d-l amphetamine mixture in peri-adolescent rhesus monkeys: Effects on physiology, behavior, and dopamine system development. *Neurpsychophamacology* 37: 2566-2579.

Tuckman, A. (2012, October). Organizing the ADHD brain: It's all about executive functions. *Attention*, 19 (4): 20-22.

Wilens, T.E., & Spencer, T.J. (2010). Understanding attention-deficit/hyperactivity disorder from childhood to adulthood. *Postgraduate Medicine* 122(5): 97-109.

Wolraich, M. L., Hannah, J.N., Pinnock, T.Y., Baumgaertel, A., & Brown, J. (1996). Comparison of diagnostic criteria for attention deficit hyperactivity disorder in a county-wide sample. *Journal of the American Academy of Child and Adolescent Psychiatry* 35: 3.

MSI PRESS BOOKS
ON PARENTING

10 Quick Homework Tips (Alder & Trombly)

108 Yoga and Self-Care Practices for Busy Mamas (Gentile)

365 Teacher Secrets for Parents: Fun Ways to Help Your Child Succeed in Elementary School (Alder & Trombly)

Choice and Structure for Children with Autism: Getting through the Long Days of Quarantine (McNeil)

Clean Your Plate! 13 Things That Good Parents Say That Ruin Kids' Lives (Bayardelle)

Everybody's Little Book of Everyday Prayers (MacGregor)

Girl, You Got This! A Fitness Trainer's Personal Strategies for Transitioning into Motherhood (Renz)

How to Be a Good Mommy When You're Sick: A Guide to Motherhood with Chronic Illness (Graves)

I Love My Kids, But I Don't Always Like Them: Expert Advice for Parents of Challenging Children (Bagdade)

Lamentations of the Heart Mingled with Peace and Joy [loss of a child] (Wells-Smith)

Lessons of Labor: One Woman's Self-Discovery through Birth and Motherhood (Aziz)

Life after Losing a Child (Romer and Young)

Noah's New Puppy [helping children understand parents with PTSD] (Rice, Rice, & Henderson)

One Simple Text.... The Lize Marks Story (Shaw & Brown)

Parenting in a Pandemic (Bayardelle)

Soccer Is Fun without Parents (Jonas)

Understanding the Challenge of "No" for Children with Autism: Improving Communication, Increasing Positivity, Enhancing Relationships (McNeil)